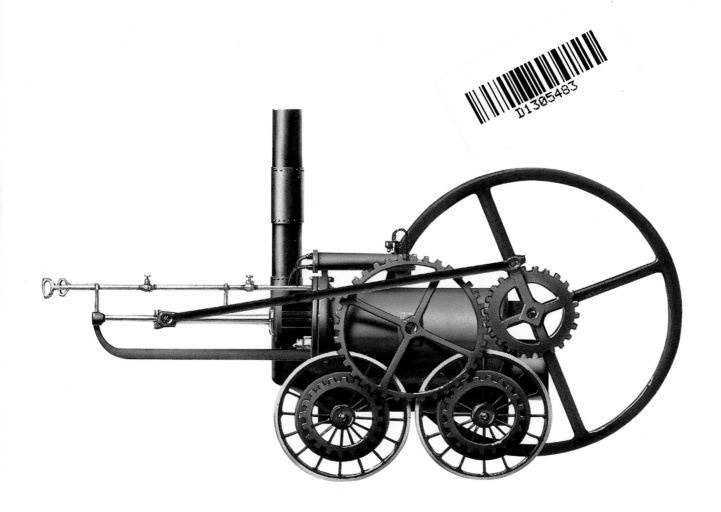

# Dictionary of
# Forces, Matter, and Energy

By Leslie Garrett

CELEBRATION PRESS
Pearson Learning Group

The following people from **Pearson Learning Group**
have contributed to the development of this product:

Joan Mazzeo, Dorothea Fox **Design** | **Editorial** Leslie Feierstone Barna, Cindy Kane
Christine Fleming **Marketing** | **Publishing Operations** Jennifer Van Der Heide
**Production** Laura Benford-Sullivan
**Content Area Consultants** Dr. Amy Rabb-Liu and Dr. Charles Liu

The following people from **DK** have
contributed to the development of this product:

**Art Director** Rachael Foster

Martin Wilson **Managing Art Editor** | **Managing Editor** Marie Greenwood
Jill Plank, Jane Tetzlaff **Design** | **Editorial** Louise Pritchard, Hannah Wilson
Helen McFarland **Picture Research** | **Production** Gordana Simakovic
Richard Czapnik, Andy Smith **Cover Design** | **DTP** David McDonald
**Consultant** David Glover

**Dorling Kindersley would like to thank:** Shirley Cachia and Rose Horridge in the DK Picture Library; Kath Northam for additional design work; Johnny Pau for additional cover design work; and models Kayude Adeniran, Chanele Dandridge, Kwade Davis, and Ayshe Khan.

**Picture Credits:** New reproductions of Beatrix Potter's illustrations copyright © Frederick Warne & Co., 2002. Beatrix Potter's original text and illustrations copyright © Frederick Warne & Co., 1902, 1903, 1906, 1907, 1908, 1946, 1955, 1968, 1972. Frederick Warne is the owner of all rights, copyrights and trademarks in the Beatrix Potter character names and illustrations. Frederick Warne & Co.: 1t, 2bl, 3cl, 3cr, 3br, 4tr, 4bl, 4br, 5br, 5l, 6cl, 6c, 6bl, 7c, 7bl, 7br, 8cl, 8bl; courtesy of the Beatrix Potter Society 1c; courtesy of the National Trust 7cr; courtesy of a Private Collector 2c, 5r; courtesy of the Victoria and Albert Museum 4cl, 8r; courtesy of the Warne Archive 3tr, 6r. Cover: Frederick Warne & Co.: front br, front c, back bl, back tc, back tr; courtesy of the Victoria and Albert Museum front l.

All other images: DK Dorling Kindersley © 2005. For further information see www.dkimages.com

ISBN: 0-7652-5238-4

Color reproduction by Colourscan, Singapore
Printed in the United States of America
5 6 7 8 9 10   08 07 06

1-800-321-3106
www.pearsonlearning.com

# Contents

# How to Use This Book

The *Dictionary of Forces, Matter, and Energy* is divided into sections called entries. All the entries in this dictionary are related to the science concepts of force, matter, and energy. The words appear in alphabetical order. Guide words can help you locate the correct page quickly.

## Each entry consists of
- an entry word in bold type
- the pronunciation in parentheses
- an abbreviation in italics that indicates the part of speech
- the word's definition or definitions

Some entries include photographs to illustrate the concepts.

*guide words*     *entry word*     *pronunciation*     *See also directs you to a related entry.*

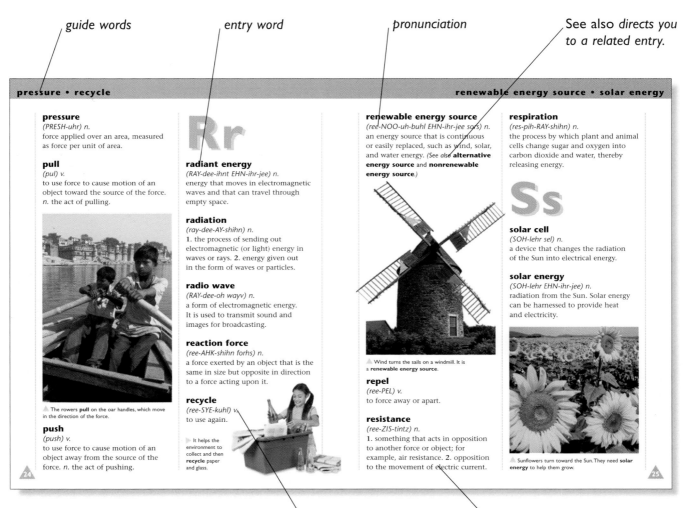

*part of speech of entry word*     *definition or definitions*

---

**pressure · recycle**

**pressure**
(PRESH-uhr) *n.*
force applied over an area, measured as force per unit of area.

**pull**
(pul) *v.*
to use force to cause motion of an object toward the source of the force. *n.* the act of pulling.

The rowers **pull** on the oar handles, which move in the direction of the force.

**push**
(push) *v.*
to use force to cause motion of an object away from the source of the force. *n.* the act of pushing.

**Rr**

**radiant energy**
(RAY-dee-ihnt EHN-ihr-jee) *n.*
energy that moves in electromagnetic waves and that can travel through empty space.

**radiation**
(ray-dee-AY-shihn) *n.*
1. the process of sending out electromagnetic (or light) energy in waves or rays. 2. energy given out in the form of waves or particles.

**radio wave**
(RAY-dee-oh wayv) *n.*
a form of electromagnetic energy. It is used to transmit sound and images for broadcasting.

**reaction force**
(ree-AHK-shihn forhs) *n.*
a force exerted by an object that is the same in size but opposite in direction to a force acting upon it.

**recycle**
(ree-SYE-kuhl) *v.*
to use again.

It helps the environment to collect and then **recycle** paper and glass.

**renewable energy source · solar energy**

**renewable energy source**
(ree-NOO-uh-buhl EHN-ihr-jee sors) *n.*
an energy source that is continuous or easily replaced, such as wind, solar, and water energy. (*See also* **alternative energy source** and **nonrenewable energy source**.)

Wind turns the sails on a windmill. It is a **renewable energy source**.

**repel**
(ree-PEL) *v.*
to force away or apart.

**resistance**
(ree-ZIS-tintz) *n.*
1. something that acts in opposition to another force or object; for example, air resistance. 2. opposition to the movement of electric current.

**respiration**
(res-pih-RAY-shihn) *n.*
the process by which plant and animal cells change sugar and oxygen into carbon dioxide and water, thereby releasing energy.

**Ss**

**solar cell**
(SOH-lehr sel) *n.*
a device that changes the radiation of the Sun into electrical energy.

**solar energy**
(SOH-lehr EHN-ihr-jee) *n.*
radiation from the Sun. Solar energy can be harnessed to provide heat and electricity.

Sunflowers turn toward the Sun. They need **solar energy** to help them grow.

24     25

# Introduction

The words *forces*, *matter*, and *energy* are often associated with science, particularly physics. Physics is the branch of science that examines matter, energy, force, and motion. The energy of the Sun heats Earth. The appliances in your home use electrical energy.

When you talk, you are producing sound energy. When you push or pull something, you exert a force. The force of Earth's gravity is always present, pulling everything toward Earth's center. Every gas, liquid, and solid on Earth is a type of matter. Virtually everything you do, say, see, or touch involves force, matter, and energy.

Life consists of a series of energy transactions. Energy is transferred from one object to another, and transformed from one form, or type of matter, to another. Force starts things moving, changes the way they move, and stops them from moving. Energy and force are always interacting and changing matter. Without force and energy, nothing much would ever happen!

▶ A boy performs a simple experiment to observe motion.

# Aa

## acceleration
*(ak-sel-uh-RAY-shuhn) n.*
the rate of change in speed or
direction of a moving object.

▲ **Acceleration** is required to make the car go faster.

## action force
*(AHK-shihn forhs) n.*
the initial force exerted by one
object on another object. *(See also*
**reaction force**.*)*

## air pressure
*(ayr PRESH-uhr) n.*
the force or weight of the atmosphere
on a unit of area, such as Earth's
surface.

## alternative energy source
*(ahl-TIR-nah-tihv EHN-ihr-jee sors) n.*
a renewable energy source, such as
the Sun, wind, tides, or waves. It is
a source of energy that is less harmful
to the environment than fossil fuels.
*(See also* **renewable energy source**.*)*

▲ Wind is an **alternative energy source**. Windmills
convert wind power into electrical energy.

## ampere
*(AM-pihr) n.*
the basic unit used to measure electric
current (abbreviation: amp).

# atom

*(AT-um) n.*

the smallest particle of an element that has the chemical properties of that element. It is considered the building block of matter and consists of a positively charged nucleus, or center, orbited by negatively charged electrons. The nucleus is made of neutrons, which have no electrical charge, and protons, which are positively charged.

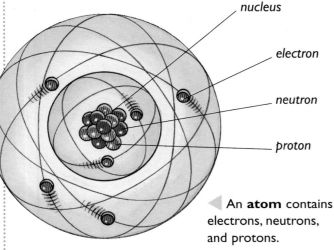

nucleus

electron

neutron

proton

◀ An **atom** contains electrons, neutrons, and protons.

# attract

*(ah-TRAHKT) v.*

to exert a pulling force on another body.

▶ An electrostatic force causes this amber earring to **attract** a feather.

# Bb

# battery

*(BAT-uh-ree) n.*

a device that uses chemicals to produce electric current. It is made up of cells in which chemicals react to convert chemical energy into electrical energy. *(See also* **cell***.)*

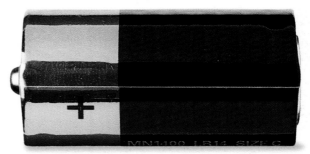

▲ A **battery** is a portable source of electrical energy. It can be used to power a flashlight, for example.

# biogas

*(BYE-oh-gahs) n.*

a mixture of methane and carbon dioxide gases produced by the decay of organic waste matter, or biomass, and used as a fuel. *(See also* **biomass***.)*

# biomass

*(BYE-oh-mas) n.*

a renewable energy source derived from organic materials, such as wood, grains, grass, and animal waste. Burning biomass fuels adds little or no carbon dioxide to the atmosphere. Biomass energy is used for heating, cooking, transportation, and electric power production.

## buoyancy

*(BOI-ihn-see) n.*

the ability of an object to float on the surface of a liquid or in gases.

▲ This child uses a rubber ring for **buoyancy**.

# Cc

## calorie

*(KAL-uh-ree) n.*

1. a unit of heat energy that measures the amount of heat needed to raise the temperature of 1 gram of water by 1 degree centigrade. 2. a unit that measures the energy value of foods (abbreviation: Cal).

## cell

*(sehl) n.*

the part of a battery in which chemical energy is converted to electrical energy. *(See also* **battery***.)*

## charge

*(chahrj) v.*

to supply with electrical or chemical energy. *(See also* **electric charge***.)*

▲ You can **charge** a balloon with electrical energy if you rub it on your hair or clothes.

## chemical bond

*(KEM-ih-kuhl bond) n.*

force of attraction that holds atoms together.

## chemical energy

*(KEM-ih-kuhl EHN-ihr-jee) n.*

energy released when materials take part in chemical reactions, such as combustion.

## circuit

*(SIHR-kiht) n.*

a closed path or loop, through which an electric current can flow.

## coal

*(kohl) n.*

a hard, black flammable rock formed when layers of organic matter, minerals, and other materials were buried over time and changed by extreme heat and pressure; also a fossil fuel that can be burned to release stored energy.

**piece of coal**

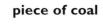

▲ This power station burns **coal** to generate electricity.

## combustion

*(kum-BUS-chihn) n.*

a process in which a substance burns rapidly when it reacts with the oxygen in the air.

## conduction

*(kuhn-DUHK-shuhn) n.*

the transfer of heat, electricity, or other energy through a substance as a result of the collision of particles.

▶ The **conduction** of electricity takes place when electricity passes through the metal screw from the battery to the light.

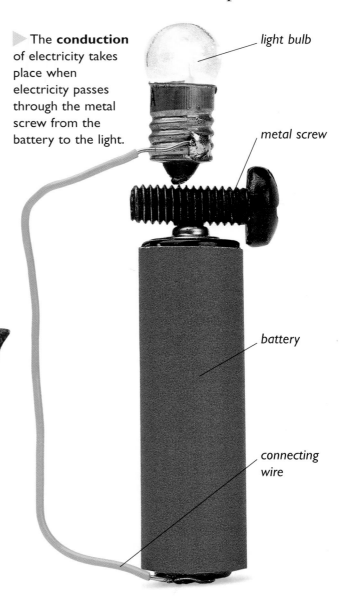

light bulb

metal screw

battery

connecting wire

## conductor

*(kuhn-DUK-tor) n.*

a substance, body, or system that allows heat, electricity, or another form of energy to flow through it. Metals such as copper and aluminum are often used as conductors of electricity.

### conservation
*(kahn-sihr-VAY-shuhn) n.*
the protection and care of natural resources so they will last longer. Recycling is one form of conservation of natural resources.

### conservation of energy
*(kahn-sihr-VAY-shihn uhv EHN-ihr-jee) n.*
the principle that energy can never be created or destroyed; it can only be changed from one form to another. Whenever energy is converted from one form to another, the total amount of energy at the end is the same as it was at the beginning.

▲ Riding a bicycle is an example of **conservation of energy.** The energy transferred from the rider's muscles to the pedals is equal to the sum of the mechanical energy of the bicycle's motion and the heat caused by friction and air resistance.

### convection
*(kuhn-VEK-shuhn) n.*
heat energy transfer by the movement of heated gases or liquids.

▲ **Convection** currents transfer heat energy throughout a heated liquid. As a liquid is warmed, it expands and rises from the base of the container. Cooler liquid sinks to take its place. Colored dye shows how the liquid moves and mixes.

### current
*(KER-ihnt) n.*
a flow of electricity.

## Dd

### density
*(DEN-sih-tee) n.*
the amount of matter in a certain volume of an object. Two objects that are exactly the same size can have different densities. The object with the higher density would have more mass and would weigh more than the object with the lower density.

# Ee

## electric charge
*(ih-LEK-trihk charj) n.*
the amount of electricity in an object, resulting from a gain or loss of electrons.

filament

▶ The flow of **electric charge** through the light bulb filament is an **electric current**.

## electric current
*(ih-LEK-trihk KER-ihnt) n.*
a flow of electric charge.

## electrical energy
*(ih-LEK-trih-kuhl EHN-ihr-jee) n.*
a form of energy carried by moving electrical charges.

## electricity
*(ih-lek-TRIHS-ih-tee) n.*
a form of energy that involves charged particles. It can be produced by chemical changes (as in a battery), by friction, or by induction (as in a generator). When the particles are moving in a circuit, it is called electric current; when the electrical charge is not moving, it is called static electricity. *(See also* **static electricity**.*)*

▲ A bolt of lightning is a huge spark of **electricity**. It is more powerful than the electricity used in buildings.

## electromagnetic radiation
*(ih-lek-troh-mag-NET-ihk ray-dee-AY-shuhn) n.*
energy that travels through space in the form of waves as a result of the motion of electric charges.

## electromagnetism
*(ih-lek-troh-MAG-nih-tiz-ihm) n.*
magnetism caused by an electric charge in motion.

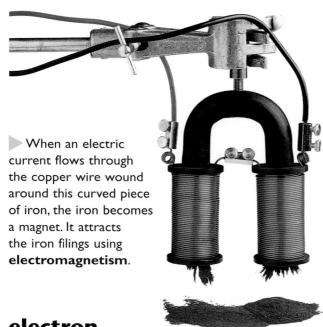

When an electric current flows through the copper wire wound around this curved piece of iron, the iron becomes a magnet. It attracts the iron filings using **electromagnetism**.

## electron
*(ih-LEK-trohn) n.*
a tiny particle found in atoms that carries a negative charge. *(See also **atom**.)*

## element
*(EL-ih-mihnt) n.*
a substance made up of atoms that have an identical number of protons in each nucleus. Elements cannot be broken down into different substances by using normal chemical means.

## energy
*(EHN-ihr-jee) n.*
the ability to cause changes in matter. There are two basic kinds of energy: kinetic energy and potential energy. These kinds of energy can take various forms, such as heat and light. *(See also **kinetic energy** and **potential energy**.)*

## energy efficiency
*(EHN-ihr-jee ih-FISH-ihn-see) n.*
the ratio of useful work performed to the total energy used or required to perform it.

## engine
*(EHN-jin) n.*
a machine that generates motion and does work by converting one type of energy into another type of energy.

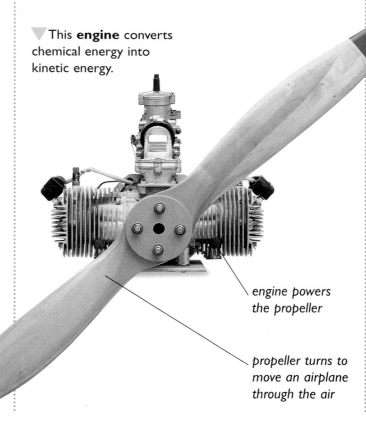

This **engine** converts chemical energy into kinetic energy.

engine powers the propeller

propeller turns to move an airplane through the air

# Ff

## fission

*(FISH-ihn) n.*

the act of splitting something into parts. Nuclear fission involves the splitting of the nucleus of an element, such as uranium or plutonium, resulting in a huge energy release. *(See also* **nuclear energy***.)*

## float

*(floht) v.*

to rest at the surface of a liquid.

◀ An unpeeled lemon will **float** in water. A peeled lemon will sink.

*lemon with peel*

*peeled lemon*

## food

*(food) n.*

any part of an animal or plant taken in by a living thing and used for growth, energy, and other vital processes.

## force

*(forhs) n.*

an influence, often a push or pull, that makes something move or stop, or changes the speed or direction of something that is already moving.

▶ Pushing the ball applies a **force** that causes it to move.

## fossil fuel

*(FAHS-uhl fyool) n.*

a natural fuel found in the ground and formed over millions of years from the remains of plants and animals.

## frequency

*(FREE-kwihn-see) n.*

the number of times a complete cycle of vibrations or waves occurs per second. It is measured in hertz (Hz), or cycles per second. For example, as a pendulum swings, the number of back-and-forth swings in a certain length of time is the frequency.

## friction

*(FRIHK-shihn) n.*

the resistance caused by rubbing one object or substance against another. Friction slows objects down and produces heat.

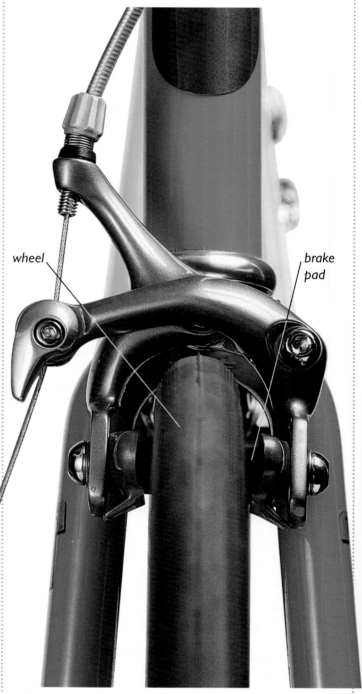

wheel

brake pad

**Friction** between the brake pads and the wheel causes the bike to stop.

pendulum at the end of its swing

The rate at which the backward-and-forward swing of a pendulum is repeated is its **frequency**.

# fuel

*(fyool) n.*

any substance burned to release stored energy and produce heat or light.

▲ A rocket burns **fuel** as it blasts off into space.

# fuse

*(fyooz) n.*

a safety device consisting of a piece of easily melted wire that will break an electric circuit if too much current passes through.

# fusion

*(FYOO-zhihn) n.*

the combining of nuclei of certain atoms to form a heavier nucleus, resulting in the release of a huge amount of energy. (*See also* **nuclear energy**.)

# Gg

# gas

*(gahs) n.*

one of three states of matter. Gas has a form similar to air and the ability to spread out to fill any available space. (*See also* **matter**.)

# generator

*(JEN-uhr-ayt-ihr) n.*

a device that uses electromagnetism to convert motion or mechanical energy into electrical energy.

# geothermal energy

*(jee-oh-THER-mahl EHN-ihr-jee) n.*

a form of energy produced from the natural heat of Earth.

# gravity

*(GRAV-ih-tee) n.*

the force that causes all objects in the universe to be pulled toward one another. Gravity keeps all the planets in our solar system moving around the Sun. It is the force that holds things on Earth close to Earth's surface.

▶ **Gravity** causes the glass to fall.

### greenhouse effect
*(GREEN-howz ih-FEKT) n.*
the process by which gases, mainly carbon dioxide and water vapor, keep planets such as Earth warmer by trapping heat and preventing it from escaping into outer space.

## Hh

### heat
*(heet) n.*
a form of energy produced by the random motion of molecules in a substance. Heat can be transferred to another object by conduction, convection, or radiation. It can also be transformed into other types of energy. *(See also* **conduction**, **convection**, *and* **radiation**.*)*

The colors in this special photograph show **heat** escaping from the surface of a house. The red areas are the warmest.

### hydraulic
*(hye-DRAH-lihk) adj.*
operated, generated, or brought about by means of a liquid, such as water, moving under pressure.

### hydroelectric energy
*(hye-droh-ih-LEK-trihk EHN-ihr-jee) n.*
a source of energy in which electricity is generated through the use of water power; an alternative to fossil fuel.

Water from this dam falls through a turbine, which drives a generator to produce **hydroelectric energy**.

## hydrogen

*(HYE-droh-jen) n.*

an odorless, colorless, tasteless, highly flammable gas that is the simplest and lightest element. The nuclei of hydrogen atoms are fused together deep inside the Sun to produce huge amounts of energy.

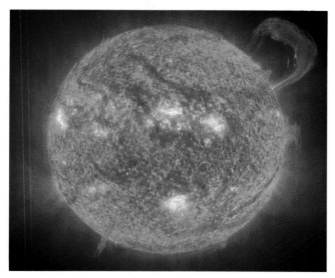

▲ The Sun is made mostly of **hydrogen**. Fusion of hydrogen nuclei produces heat and light energy.

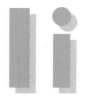

## inertia

*(in-ER-shuh) n.*

the tendency of an object to stay at rest or to continue moving in a straight line unless an outside force causes a change. Inertia causes an object to resist changes in its motion. Mass is related to an object's inertia; the greater the mass, the greater the inertia.

## input

*(IHN-put) n.*

something that is put into a machine or system, such as power, energy, a signal, or information.

## insulator

*(IHN-suh-lay-tuhr) n.*

material through which heat, electricity, or sound does not pass easily.

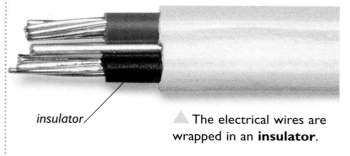

*insulator*

▲ The electrical wires are wrapped in an **insulator**.

## joule

*(jool) n.*

a metric unit used to measure work or energy; named after James Joule, who was the first to measure the rate at which mechanical energy can be converted into heat.

▶ The **joule** was named after James Joule, an English scientist.

# Kk

## kilowatt
*(KIHL-uh-waht) n.*
a unit used to measure large amounts of electric power and equal to 1,000 watts. *(See also* **watt.***)*

## kilowatt-hour
*(KIHL-uh-waht owr) n.*
a unit of electrical energy equal to the use of 1,000 watts of energy for one hour.

▲ A toaster running for an hour would use about 1 **kilowatt-hour** of energy.

◀ An electric meter measures the amount of electrical energy used in **kilowatt-hours**.

## kinetic energy
*(kih-NET-ihk EHN-ihr-jee) n.*
the energy of a moving object, which depends on the object's speed and mass; the faster an object moves and the more mass it has, the more kinetic energy it has.

# Ll

## lever
*(LEHV-ehr) n.*
a simple machine consisting of a bar that turns about a fixed point called a fulcrum and that, when acted upon by force, can move a load or decrease resistance. Examples of levers include seesaws, scissors, pliers, nutcrackers, and tongs.

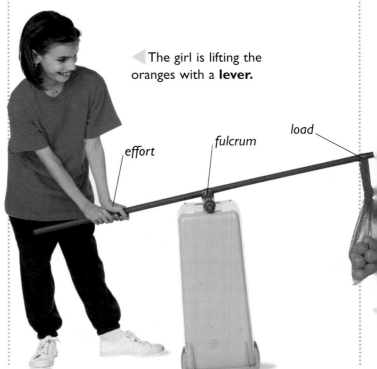

◀ The girl is lifting the oranges with a **lever.**

effort

fulcrum

load

## light
*(lyt) n.*
visible electromagnetic radiation that travels through a vacuum at about 186,000 miles per second, faster than anything else in the universe.

White **light** is a mixture of colors. A prism splits light into a band of colors called a spectrum.

## lightning
*(LYT-nihng) n.*
a flash of light caused by the movement of electric charges between two clouds, a cloud and the ground, or between objects on the ground, or two parts of a single cloud.

## liquid
*(LIHK-wihd) n.*
one of three states of matter. Liquid has a definite volume but no definite shape. *(See also* **matter**.*)*

## machine
*(mah-SHEEN) n.*
a device made up of fixed or movable parts that makes a task easier or faster by changing the amount or direction of force needed to do the task.

## magnet
*(MAG-niht) n.*
a material, such as iron, that attracts and repels with a magnetic force.

A **magnet** attracts metal paper clips.

## magnetism
*(MAG-nih-tiz-ihm) n.*
a type of force produced by magnets or magnetized objects.

## mass
*(mahss) n.*
a measure of the amount of matter in an object.

## matter
*(MAHT-ehr) n.*
anything that has mass. The three most common states of matter on Earth are liquid, solid, and gas.

### mechanical energy
*(mih-KAN-ih-kuhl EHN-ihr-jee) n.*
energy that an object has as a result of its motion, position, or condition; related to the kinetic energy of moving objects.

In a moving roller coaster, **mechanical energy** is transformed back and forth from the form of potential, or stored, energy to the form of kinetic energy.

### microwave
*(MYE-kroh-wayv) n.*
a type of electromagnetic radiation; short radio waves, which are used in radar, communications, and cooking.

### molecule
*(MAHL-ih-kyool) n.*
the smallest particle of a substance that possesses all the chemical properties of the substance. A molecule is made up of two or more atoms.

### motion
*(MOH-shihn) n.*
movement or change in position of an object.

▶ A gyroscope has circular **motion.**

## Nn

### natural gas
*(NACH-uhr-uhl gahs) n.*
a combustible gas found naturally in Earth's crust and used as a fossil fuel.

### natural resource
*(NACH-uhr-uhl REE-zors) n.*
material found in nature that can be used by living things.

## newton
*(NOO-tihn) n.*
the unit in the metric system that is used to measure force; named after the famous scientist Sir Isaac Newton.

▶ Sir Isaac Newton was an English scientist who studied motion and gravity. The **newton**, a unit of force, is named after him.

## Newton's first law of motion
*(NOO-tihnz ferst law uhv MOH-shihn) n.*
a law that states that an object at rest will not move unless a force acts on it. Likewise, an object that is moving in a straight line will continue to do so unless an outside force acts on it.

## Newton's second law of motion
*(NOO-tihnz SEH-kihnd law uhv MOH-shihn) n.*
a law that states how an object's acceleration depends on the mass of the object and the amount and direction of the force acting on it.

## Newton's third law of motion
*(NOO-tihnz therd law uhv MOH-shihn) n.*
a law that states that when one object exerts a force upon another, the second object exerts an equal and opposite force upon the first one; for every action, there is an equal and opposite reaction.

## nonrenewable energy source
*(non-ree-NOO-uh-buhl EHN-ihr-jee sors) n.*
an energy source that is very hard to replace, such as fossil fuels. Examples of nonrenewable energy sources include coal, oil, and natural gas. These release heat when they are burned. *(See also* **renewable energy source**.*)*

▲ Petroleum, or crude oil, is a **nonrenewable energy source**. It is extracted by drilling below Earth's surface.

### nuclear energy
*(NOO-klee-uhr EHN-ihr-jee) n.*
a form of energy produced when the nucleus of an atom splits or when the nuclei of two or more atoms join together to form one atom. (See also **fission** and **fusion**.)

### nucleus
*(NOO-klee-ihs) n.*
the central part of an atom that is made up of positively charged protons, and neutrons that have no charge. The nucleus makes up almost all of the mass of an atom. *pl.* **nuclei** *(NOO-klee-eye)*

## Oo

### oil
*(oyl) n.*
a kind of fossil fuel; a liquid or easily liquified material that burns easily and does not dissolve in water but does dissolve in organic solvents.

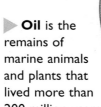

▶ **Oil** is the remains of marine animals and plants that lived more than 200 million years ago.

### output
*(OWT-poot) n.*
the energy or power produced by a machine or system.

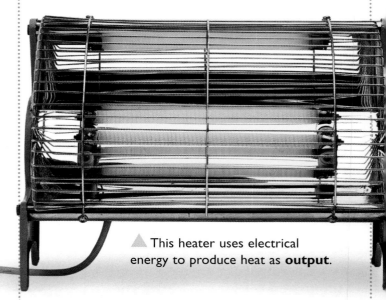

▲ This heater uses electrical energy to produce heat as **output**.

## Pp

### particle
*(PAR-tih-kul) n.*
a very tiny piece of matter.

### photosynthesis
*(foht-oh-SIHN-thuh-sihs) n.*
the process by which green plants, algae, or other organisms, use the Sun's energy to make sugar from water and carbon dioxide.

▶ **Photosynthesis** occurs in the cells of green plants, algae, and other organisms that contain chlorophyll.

## pole
*(pohl) n.*
either of two ends of a magnet where magnetism is the strongest.

## pollution
*(puh-LOO-shin) n.*
harmful substances that damage or poison the air, land, or water. Some pollution comes from burning fossil fuels.

Air **pollution** in Paris, France, causes smog to hang over the city.

## position
*(poh-ZISH-ihn) n.*
an object's location, or place, in time and space.

## potential energy
*(poh-TEN-shuhl EHN-ihr-jee) n.*
energy stored in an object due to the object's position, condition, or composition.

## power
*(POW-er) n.*
the rate at which work is done or energy is produced. Usually measured in work per unit of time, such as watt, kilowatt, or megawatt.

## power plant
*(POW-er plant) n.*
group of buildings where electrical power is produced and sent to places that need electricity, such as homes, stores, and industries. Nuclear power plants use nuclear fuel, such as uranium, whereas other power plants use fossil fuels or water.

This nuclear **power plant** is in Germany.

## pressure
*(PRESH-uhr) n.*
force applied over an area, measured as force per unit of area.

## pull
*(pul) v.*
to use force to cause motion of an object toward the source of the force. *n.* the act of pulling.

▲ The rowers **pull** on the oar handles, which move in the direction of the force.

## push
*(push) v.*
to use force to cause motion of an object away from the source of the force. *n.* the act of pushing.

# Rr

## radiant energy
*(RAY-dee-ihnt EHN-ihr-jee) n.*
energy that moves in electromagnetic waves and that can travel through empty space.

## radiation
*(ray-dee-AY-shihn) n.*
1. the process of sending out electromagnetic (or light) energy in waves or rays. 2. energy given out in the form of waves or particles.

## radio wave
*(RAY-dee-oh wayv) n.*
a form of electromagnetic energy. It is used to transmit sound and images for broadcasting.

## reaction force
*(ree-AHK-shihn forhs) n.*
a force exerted by an object that is the same in size but opposite in direction to a force acting upon it.

## recycle
*(ree-SYE-kuhl) v.*
to use again.

▶ It helps the environment to collect and then **recycle** paper and glass.

## renewable energy source
*(ree-NOO-uh-buhl EHN-ihr-jee sors) n.*
an energy source that is continuous or easily replaced, such as wind, solar, and water energy. *(See also* **alternative energy source** and **nonrenewable energy source***.)*

▲ Wind turns the sails on a windmill. It is a **renewable energy source**.

## repel
*(ree-PEL) v.*
to force away or apart.

## resistance
*(ree-ZIS-tintz) n.*
1. something that acts in opposition to another force or object; for example, air resistance. 2. opposition to the movement of electric current.

## respiration
*(res-pih-RAY-shihn) n.*
the process by which plant and animal cells change sugar and oxygen into carbon dioxide and water, thereby releasing energy.

# Ss

## solar cell
*(SOH-lehr sel) n.*
a device that changes the radiation of the Sun into electrical energy.

## solar energy
*(SOH-lehr EHN-ihr-jee) n.*
radiation from the Sun. Solar energy can be harnessed to provide heat and electricity.

▲ Sunflowers turn toward the Sun. They need **solar energy** to help them grow.

### solid
*(SOHL-ihd) n.*
one of three states of matter. A solid has a definite size and shape. *(See also* **matter***.)*

### sound
*(sownd) n.*
a form of energy produced by the vibration of molecules in air, water, or other matter; sound travels in the form of waves.

### speed
*(speed) n.*
the rate of motion, measuring how quickly an object moves over a certain distance.

### static electricity
*(STAT-ihk ih-lek-TRIS-ih-tee) n.*
electrical charges that do not flow through a conductor; can sometimes be created by rubbing two things together.

▲ **Static electricity** makes this girl's hair stand up.

### switch
*(swihch) n.*
the part of an electric circuit that controls the flow of electricity.

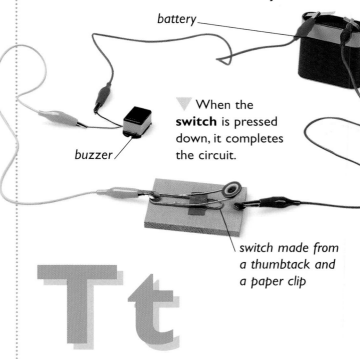

battery

buzzer

▼ When the **switch** is pressed down, it completes the circuit.

switch made from a thumbtack and a paper clip

## Tt

### temperature
*(TEM-pehr-uh-choor) n.*
how hot or cold a substance is as measured on a definite scale.

▲ This thermometer measures **temperature** in degrees Fahrenheit and degrees Celsius.

### thermal energy
*(THER-mul EHN-ihr-jee) n.*
a form of energy related to temperature that is created by the movement of atoms and molecules of matter. The higher the temperature, the greater the movement of the molecules, and the greater the thermal energy released.

## thunder
*(THUN-der) n.*
the loud noise created when the air
is quickly heated and expanded by
a lightning discharge.

## tidal energy
*(TYD-uhl EHN-ihr-jee) n.*
a form of energy produced on Earth by
the rise and fall of the ocean's tides.

▲ This dam on the Rance River in France produces
**tidal energy** when water flows through twenty-four
turbines.

## transfer of energy
*(TRANS-fuhr uhv EHN-ihr-jee) n.*
the movement of energy from one object
or place to another. *(See also* **work***.)*

## transformation of energy
*(trans-fuhr-MAY-shuhn uhv
EHN-ihr-jee) n.*
the changing of one form of energy
into another form.

▲ Lighting a match shows the **transformation of
energy**. Chemical energy changes to light and heat.

## turbine
*(TER-bihn) n.*
a device that turns a shaft that can
drive a generator and produce
electricity; often powered by the
energy of steam or water that passes
through it.

▲ **Turbines** are located in power plants.

# Uu

## ultrasound
*(UL-trah-sownd) n.*
sound waves with frequencies above
the range of human hearing.

### ultraviolet ray
*(ul-tra-VYE-uh-let ray) n.*
invisible electromagnetic radiation with more energy than light, but less energy than X-rays. Ultraviolet lamps have many uses, including the sterilization of hospital equipment.

# Vv

### velocity
*(veh-LAHS-ih-tee) n.*
a measure of the speed of an object's motion in a specific direction.

▶ The **velocity** of this rocket is more than 31,000 miles per hour away from Earth.

### volt
*(vohlt) n.*
a unit of measurement of electrical energy per unit of charge. Voltage is somewhat like the pressure of the flow of electrical energy.

### volume
*(VOL-yoom) n.*
1. the amount of space occupied by a certain amount of matter. 2. the loudness or softness of a sound.

▶ The **volume** of a quantity of liquid can be measured by pouring it into a measuring cup.

# Ww

### watt
*(waht) n.*
a metric unit that measures power, such as electrical power; equal to 1 joule of work performed per second; named after James Watt. (See *also* **kilowatt**.)

## wave energy
*(wayv EHN-ihr-jee) n.*
a renewable energy source that extracts the energy stored in ocean waves.

▲ Surfers like to ride powerful waves. Ocean waves can also be used to provide **wave energy**.

## wavelength
*(WAYV-lengkth) n.*
the distance between the crest of one wave and the crest of the next wave.

## weight
*(wayt) n.*
a measure of the force that gravity exerts on an object's mass. Some units of measurement commonly used to describe weight are *pound* and *newton*.

## wind energy
*(wind EHN-ihr-jee) n.*
a renewable energy source that comes from the wind.

## wood
*(wood) n.*
the hard, fibrous material under the bark of a tree or shrub, commonly used as fuel.

▼ **Wood** burns easily, so it is a useful fuel.

## work
*(work) n.*
the amount of energy transferred when a force is moved through a distance; the amount of energy involved in completing a particular task.

## X-ray
*(EKS-ray) n.*
electromagnetic radiation that can penetrate body tissue and other substances and make a photographic image.

# Timeline of Major Discoveries

Countless people have contributed to the study of forces, matter, and energy. A timeline of major discoveries could begin 4,500 years ago, when Egyptian builders harnessed the energy of people and simple machines to construct the huge Pyramids of Giza. This timeline begins in the Renaissance, the age of William Gilbert, Galileo, and other giants of science. In the words of Isaac Newton, all later scientists are "standing on the shoulders" of these giants.

## 1600
William Gilbert publishes his findings about magnetism, including the idea that Earth is like a huge magnet with magnetic poles near the North and South Poles.

## 1800
Alessandro Volta makes the first battery.

**Alessandro Volta's battery**

## 1820
Hans Christian Oersted proves that electricity and magnetism are related, beginning the study of electromagnetism.

This is the document in which Hans Christian Oersted published his discovery about electricity and magnetism.

## 1847
Hermann Helmholtz outlines the law of conservation of energy.

**statue of Albert Einstein**

## 1905
Albert Einstein introduces the theory of relativity.

## 1911
Ernest Rutherford discovers that atoms have a nucleus, or center.

## 1913
Niels Bohr presents the modern theory of the atom.

## 1938
Otto Hahn and Fritz Strassman divide the nucleus of an atom (nuclear fission), beginning the nuclear age.

## 1942
Enrico Fermi and Leo Szilard produce the first nuclear chain reaction.

## 1945
The first atomic bomb is exploded in New Mexico.

## 1632

Galileo Galilei shows that objects made of the same material fall at the same speed regardless of their weight.

**Isaac Newton**

## 1687

Isaac Newton explains his three laws of motion.

## 1746

Benjamin Franklin begins his electrical experiments to prove that lightning is a form of electricity.

**statue of Benjamin Franklin**

## 1769

James Watt improves the steam engine, making it more efficient.

## 1864

James Clerk Maxwell publishes his theory that light is an electromagnetic wave.

## 1895

Wilhelm Roentgen discovers X-rays.

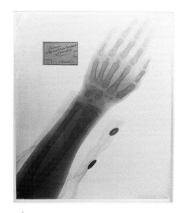

▲ This X-ray is an exhibit from the International Museum of Surgical Science.

**Marie Curie**

## 1898

Marie and Pierre Curie announce their discovery of radium, an element with strong radioactive properties.

**Maria Goeppert Mayer**

## 1963

Maria Goeppert Mayer is a co-winner of the 1963 Nobel Prize in Physics for her investigation of the model of the nucleus of the atom.

## 1974

The world's largest particle accelerator at the time is opened at the University of British Columbia in Canada.

## 1999

A car maker unveils the first drivable car powered by non-polluting hydrogen fuel cells.

# Units of Measurement

Scientists around the world use units from the metric system, such as meters, grams, and liters, to measure forces, matter, and energy. Because metric units increase or decrease in size by multiples of 10, the metric system is simple to use and is understood by scientists everywhere.

| Measurement | Units | Symbol | Value |
|---|---|---|---|
| Length | millimeter | mm | |
| | centimeter | cm | 1 cm = 10 mm |
| | meter | m | 1 m = 100 cm |
| | kilometer | km | 1 km = 1,000 m |
| Mass | gram | g | |
| | kilogram | kg | 1 kg = 1,000 g |
| | metric ton | t | 1 t = 1,000 kg |
| Volume | milliliter | mL | |
| | liter | L | 1 L = 1,000 mL |
| Power | watt | W | |
| | kilowatt | kW | 1 kW = 1,000 W |
| Frequency | hertz | Hz | |
| | kilohertz | kHz | 1 kHz = 1,000 Hz |
| Energy | joule | J | |
| | kilojoule | kJ | 1 kJ = 1,000 J |
| Force | newton | N | |
| | kilonewton | kN | 1 kN = 1,000 N |